SOUNDS FROM A BEATING HEART

THE POETRY OF
LATOYA CHAVERS

First Printing 2016

ISBN-13: 978-1539991601

ISBN-10: 1539991601

Cover Design by D. Brown Productions

Table of Contents

Introduction

Thank you for your support by purchasing this book. For many years I've held my thoughts and feelings inside. Writing poetry has given me an amazing outlet to express myself in ways that one could only imagine. Writing gives me the strength and courage to release my emotions in a positive way. As you will see, at times I reflect back on the way things used to be back in the day. At times you will see the emotional rollercoaster that I've been on. At times you will see the love I felt in my heart followed by the heartbreak that came after. On this journey I opened my heart and I'm allowing you to listen to the beat.....

lant Life

You stole my freedom and shattered my life

Sold my family and cancelled my wife

Placed my clothes in the back of a jeep

Then drove me straight to Conner's street

Scratched up arms and blistered feet

Ten hours and only thirty minutes to eat

Days are high seniority while afternoons ain't it

Destroyed my life so I couldn't quit

Ninety days and you contracted me in

Leaving me stranded in this place of sin

The assembly line is where you took my soul

Leading me to a world that only plant workers know

Too Proud

I am too proud of who I am
To complain about where I came from
The life I lived made it possible for me to be where I am today

I am too proud of who I am
To walk with my head to the ground worried about what other people
think of me or have to say

I am too proud of the color of my skin
To be ashamed of how beautiful I am as a human being with a beautiful
heart

I am too proud of who I am
To stand or walk next to a person that is ashamed of me, what I look like,
or how I talk

I am too proud of who I am
To ever be ashamed of me

I am too proud of who I am
To settle for whatever life throws my way when I can step out on faith and
pursue my dreams

I am too proud of who I am
To kick another human while they're down when I can lend a helping
hand to pull them up

I am too proud of who I am
To judge another person because of who they are or what they've been
through, in life everyone struggles and everyone can succeed

I am too proud of who I am
To be ashamed of where I've been, where I am, where I'm going, or
whose going with me on this journey

I am too proud of who I am
To be ashamed of my life

I am too proud of who I am
To be ashamed of me

I am too proud of who I am
To be ashamed of you

What is Happening on Earth

Cherry blends, black and mild's, cigarettes to weed

51s, Percocet, poppin' molly and sippin' lean

Shots of Hennessey and Remy now 1738

Victoria secret pink and a bundle girls setting wedding dates

Men screwing men and women screwing women

Ménage a trois raw thinking everybody winning

Men transitioning to women while women do the same

Government bought synthetic weed is where we place the blame

Un-curable diseases with unknown names surfacing on earth

Abortion numbers decreasing cause girls trying to keep a man by giving birth

Whores are housewives on aid while real women struggle

Working hard and going to school with children to juggle

Men are no longer leading giving women no leader in the household

Money has become more important and family is now worth less than gold

Life is no longer valued on today's streets

Everyday a mother watches her child lowered six feet

You can cry inside but can't show the pain on your face

Living in hell on earth cause we killing our own race

The number of deaths rapidly increasing for women and children

Because man has changed the circumstances of the world we live in

This mess has to stop, we living in fear of our lives daily with people with no sorrow

Losing faith in God giving the devil the power to determine what happens tomorrow

Prayer is non-existent and humans have lost all hope and faith

No more sunshine just clouds and rain, love is gone leaving a world of hate

*7*ake it back

Take it back to the days of jumping rope and playing hop scotch

Those were the good times we had on my block

Down by the ocean, down by the sea

Playing games with my sisters and friends under the big red tree

Double Dutch, hide go seek, or freeze tag you're it

Jumping fences and running from dogs trying not to get bit

Bike riding on ten speeds all around the neighborhood

Take it back to the days when life meant something and was good

Trips to the corner store for a quarter juice and bag of chips

Ring pops, bubblicious, now and laters or a fun dip

Store owners knew families and made sure everybody ate

Allowed you to get food and pay for it at a later date

Shooting dice on the corner was the worst thing you'd see

Maybe a bum in the middle of the alley about to pee

Clothes passed down from generation to generation

People didn't down you for taking hammy downs or donations

Thugs were thugs and drug dealers were dealing

But no senseless killing and unnecessary stealing

Take it back to the days when babies were innocent and mothers cared

When you could play on the porch and not be scared

Summer time blazing from old schools slowly cruising down the block

The days when it was cool for young rappers to wear real clocks

Block parties with food, games and music to dance

Neighborhood watch so tight thieves didn't have a chance

Excitement, laughter, and good times happened on my street

Let's take it back to fire hydrates cooling us down from the heat

Let's take it back to neighbors being neighbors and reclaiming our streets

*D*etroit

They say the streets be talking

They say Detroit ain't the place to be

They say this city is not a safe place to live or to raise a normal family

They say Detroit is a death trap and no one can escape alive

They say get out the city and move to the suburbs in order to survive

They say Detroit is the place of burnt down houses and vacant lots

They say ain't no hope for this city or the people so just let it rot

Detroit is not perfect, there ain't a city that is

Funny how downtown is the place where rich folks are now starting to build

Move out the low class, lock up all the thugs and purchase all the land

Raising prices and taxes so high that normal people don't have a leg to stand

They say Detroit ain't the place to be

I say Detroit is the place to be and we need to take back our city

Stop running to the suburbs where for years we weren't accepted

Giving up grandfathered taxed homes to now look back and regret it

Detroit is and always will be the city you make it

Stop giving up our homes out of fear and danger and reclaim it

Detroit is a city of pride with many opportunities to grow

Stop believing the lies and use everything you know

They say the streets be talking

They say Detroit ain't the place to be

They building Detroit back up and they trying to do it without you and me

Will You

Will you accept me as I am?

Will you appreciate my helping hand?

Will you smile when I enter the room?

Will you lay with me under the moon?

Will you wipe my tears as I cry?

Will you stare in my beautiful eyes?

Will you hold me when I'm feeling weak?

Will you understand me if I cannot speak?

Will you ride with me to the mountain top?

Will you stay with me until the pain stops?

Will you be with me when the times get hard?

Will you stand as my protector, my friend, my guard?

Will you love me even when I don't love myself?

Will you give only me your heart not anyone else?

Will you love me when I feel poor, lost, and alone?

Will you be there with me or will you be gone?

Worthless

A place in my heart reserved only for him

With no space in his heart for me

A smile on my face when I think of him

Hoping he's thinking of me

Any time, any place I'll be there for him

But he never has time for me

One side of my bed I keep ready for him

No side in his bed for me

Dressed to impress and ready to go with him

He never has plans to take me

Every time the phone rings I answer for him

He just can't seem to answer for me

When he knocks on my door I open it every time for him

His has never opened up for me

I always say I love you to him

He just never says I love you to me

Inside I know I deserve more from him

But he won't give more to me

I decided today I'd close my legs to him.

Today he walked away from me

All the things I did to prove I was worth it to him

Took all my worth from me

Feeling Worthless

*B*roken Promises

You promised me your mind

Then you turned your head

All your thoughts were locked and the communication went dead

You promised me your heart

Then you took it away

Leaving me listening to your pulse as it faded away

You promised me your love

Then you kept it all to yourself

Leaving me wondering if you wanted someone else

You promised me a new life

Then you lived yours alone

By this time tomorrow

I promise I'll be gone

Defaulted Love

It's a relationship by default, you were not the first choice

Had she stayed with him and laid with him, had she never used her voice

You would be silenced, a person whom could never exist

A steel picture on the wall waiting for a frame to assist

The beauty that lies in you is hidden away from the world

Kept away as a secret knowing you could never be his girl

You will never hold his hand

You will never drive his whip

You will never be his lady

You will never take a trip

It's a relationship by default, you were not the first choice

Stop sitting back in silence, use your voice

Single

I am single by choice, not because I have to be

I am saving myself for the one that was created for me

The one that loves my spirit and can match my high

The one I can live life with before we float on clouds in the sky

The one that loves just hearing the sound of my voice

The one that walks in a room and silences all noise

This person that was created just for me

They're somewhere in the world waiting to meet

I will know it's them when their pheromones hit my nose

My knees will get weak with a slight tinkle in my toes

We'll smile at each other and hold a mysterious stare

Wondering in our minds if we've met before some where

We will part ways abruptly never uttering a word

I always turn away from the one I know I deserve

I am single by choice, not because I have to be

I just can't determine the fool from the one that was created for me

ost

Pretty little dark skinned running lost in the city

Her dude calling her on stage just to bounce her titties

To be accepted by the world she would degrade herself

Easing the pain drinking long islands, top shelf

Bands won't make her dance it was love and affection she needed

He started giving her more of what she wanted every time she pleaded

Frequent visits in the night turned to overnight stays

Watching movies in the dark eating Denny's before day

Long talks on the phone helped bring them closer

He began showing her love like there was no other

She fell in love with him and gave him her heart

He kept her believing she had a place in his heart

Controlling her mind and every move she made

She always did what he said and never disobeyed

A magnificent toy to play with when no one's around

Ashamed those that respected him would see her and frown

Beautiful in his eyes and a perfect woman to wife

Just not on this planet and not in this life

He had an image to keep with his family and friends

Never realizing how he broke the heart of his best friend

Pretty little dark skinned running lost in the city

Thought she had a friend but he was really her enemy

A diamond in the rough is what he said he found

But a painite gem is what he stomped in the ground

Weak

He sat right by her side and called her weak

She sat back silently and did not speak

He said the details of their lives would bring them closer

He revealed her secrets trying to shame her in front of others

Quietly she sat as he tried to tell them her story

Now she's questioning his truth, his lies, and his loyalty

Putting her on blast was showing his true colors

She held his secrets inside cause she promised not to tell others

Anger in his eyes as hatred covered his face

Moving closer to face her while invading her space

Losing his self-control to prove a point to someone else

Stripping himself of his title and his champions belt

The mask covering his face quickly fell to the floor

Revealing a different man she'd never seen before

Naked, scared, and feeling defeated in life

A lost soul running wildly not knowing who to fight

Tearing down his own castle and removing himself as king

Proved him not worthy and un-loyal to his queen

Weak is not she who fights to wear the crown

Weak is the dishonorable one trying to break the queen down

eartbroken

You gave pieces to me but gave it all to someone else

You walked with her proudly but placed me on a dusty shelf

You loved me in the darkness but let her shine in the light

You treated me like a side piece but respected her as your queen or wife

You watched me struggle but made a way for her to move

You made me fight for it but you moved her in to share your room

You told me to wait for your heart but you let her listen to the beat

You filled me up on the couch but made love to her on your sheets

You encouraged me to live life alone but you had her by your side

You think you keeping it 100 but to me you completely lied

You shattered my heart to pieces but you kept hers whole

You hurt me for the last time, you just killed a beautiful soul

*R*elease me

I've lost myself inside of you and would like to have me back

Release the hold you placed on me or prepare for my attack

My guards were down when you came around giving you complete control

I allowed you to break me down by giving you my heart and soul

The chance to feel loved again made the choice so easy

Realization has set in and you now need to free me

You've captured all of my energy and my body is now so weak

Return to me my mind so I can finally clearly think

I'm strong, not weak just a woman who has a heart

I need you to release me please so the beat can finally restart

It Was Me

It was me who let him in to my peaceful place

I gave him full control and the power of my personal estate

It was me that laid down while he stole my glory

I gave him my pen and he rewrote my story

It was me that took his lies and tried to make them true

I gave him my trust and placed him before you

It was me that felt you intentionally punished and failed me

I gave up all my love and you left me here empty

It was me and only me that allowed this devil in

I gave him my soul and he filled me up with sin

It is me down on my knees praying for forgiveness

I give you back the power and release my resentment

It is me standing tall and strong now believing in myself

You gave me a new day, another chance in life to better myself

Feelings

Feels like rain from a thunderstorm whipping across your face

Consuming air breathing out fire calmly with a steady pace

A small burning feeling gliding slowly inside your chest

Sharp pains of rage shooting rapidly surrounding your breast

Smoking hot lumps of coal back flipping inside your stomach

Two hundred pound weights being dropped one on each leg

> Feels like unbearable pain and long term suffering
>
> Built up frustration about to explode because you've had enough of it
>
> Let it out with a burst of flames in front of the entire world
>
> Show the strength of a strong woman, not the weakness from a scared girl
>
> Judge the case, rule in your favor, you don't need to stand trial
>
> Shout out "I am worth it" at the top of your lungs with a victorious smile

Feels like joy and happiness with a lifetime of peace of mind

No more jumping through hurdles or fighting for time

Forget settling for inconsistent pieces and momentary fun

Actions clearly demonstrate you are not the marrying one

Ignore your heart and listen to your mind

Love don't leave you lonely and continuously crying

> Feels like I'm alone in this world sinking slowly in quick sand
>
> Every ship has sailed and I'm drowning on dry land

Fighting on life support to keep the beat going on a brutally damaged heart

Just sign the papers and pull the plug, if it's meant to beat it will restart

*I*n my mind

In my mind it's

A sold out stage play with no audience viewing the performance

A one person show of a heart felt romance

A hope for love charity run with no one to donate for the cause

A hopeless romantic with only one person giving it all

In my mind it's

A monopoly game with pieces from life and money from trouble

A chess game played on a beaten down checkers board

A round of phase ten with a solitaire layout and a joker completing the set

A dice game in a court house with a judge placing the first bet

In my mind it's

A thousand Puzzle pieces hanging from a chandelier

A sink full of shattered glass on the table top ready to be served

A ceramic cup filled with beauty putting out a blazing house fire

A black shadow giving birth to hope and desire

In my mind it's

A disaster in life and love and nothing makes sense

Finish Line

Running in circles trying to get to your heart

Every day ends and I wake up back at start

Sweat beads dripping as I race to the finish line

Breathless and exhausted as I run for mine

Chasing a dream that seems out of my reach

Smiling faces in the crowd awaiting my victory speech

I can see you from here as my heart begins to race

I push harder and run faster to get closer to your face

You look at me and smile as you move back the line

The buzzer goes off and I'm out of time

I couldn't stop the tears as you yelled out give up

The world started spending as I stood there stuck

Confused and defeated trying to get what's mine

Finally realizing you are not my finish line

*N*o More

I don't want to do this anymore

I don't want to be in this space no more

Take away these feelings and discontinue this pain

Give me back my sunshine

I don't want to drown in this rain

I don't want to be here anymore

I don't want to fight no more

Take away these thoughts and empty this brain

Give me back peace of mind

I don't want to go insane

I don't want to cry anymore

I don't want to hurt no more

Take away this heartache and let the bad blood drain

Give me back good love

I don't want this pain

I don't want to do this anymore

I will not do this no more

I need you

I need you in the morning

I need you in the night

I need you to hold me

Wrapped in your arms so tight

The calm breeze of wind

That fills the room

As we lay in silence

Watching the moon

Our hearts beat as one

As the night turns to day

Wishing the moment wouldn't end

As the sun takes its place

I need you near me

I need you to stay

Holding me in your arms

Every single day

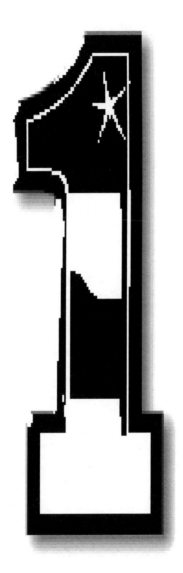

One of a Kind

Sunshine on a rainy day

Is how you make me feel when you come my way

Flowers bloom when you smile

For your love I'd walk a thousand miles

I breathe the air you breathe

I'd like to be everything you need

I'd be the razor you need to shave

If the suns too bright I'd be your shade

I'd lift you up when you're feeling down

You're the one I love to be around

You keep me safe from this cruel world

For you love I'd compete with every girl

You are the one that's always on my mind

The love we have is one of a kind

ou

You changed my life and opened a door

With every beat of my heart I wanted more

I love you and everything you bring

Making me wish I never accepted his ring

You make me feel like I've never felt

Like a heavy weight champion receiving his belt

I know what I want and the fight I'm willing to take

The sad part is you now think I was a mistake

I gave to you my heart, body and soul

Allowed you to go where no other man will ever go

I can't force myself on a man that seems so sure

But his eyes tell me that he wants more

I made the choice to keep dangling on

But it's clear to me now that I must move on

Forgetting what I found in you will be the hardest part

Just know that where I placed you is in my heart

I seal it with my blood and toss the key

The person left hurting is not you, it's me

Letting Go

When it's time to let go and move on

It hurts, it's painful and it's horribly sad

Reminiscing about all the good times and exciting adventures you had

Wondering what happened to the amazing love you felt

Confused about how you played wrong the perfect hand you were dealt

How you could fall so hard for someone living a heartbreaking lie

An untrustworthy person with no real feelings inside

A selfish human receiving satisfaction by making others cry

Breaking you down slowly and never explaining why

Best friends was our label as we laid up in the night

Just another lie made up to make your wrongs seem right

Unacceptable in every way but unconditional love is real

When your love is taken for granted tell me how it makes you feel

Best friend!

Silent Goodbye

I cried myself to sleep last night
as I laid quietly in your bed

I wrapped my arms around me tightly
wishing it were you holding me instead

One sheet and two blankets
should've kept me warm and snuggled

Your back to mine was cold as ice
with no desire from you to cuddle

You peacefully slept as I silently wept
and prayed for a simple sign

Nothing happened and nothing ever will
so I will give up and stop my trying

You will never be my woman were the words you said
but my heart didn't understand

Alone in your bed with you next to me
painted a vivid picture
my mind could finally comprehend

Home

Just bricks formed together to keep you warm and block the rain

It's a house to live in while some think a home is just the same

A place of shelter with a bed to close your eyes and rest your head

It's a meeting place for the homeless to get clothed and repeatedly fed

A pit stop for the lost ones to freshen up and have cold water to drink

It's not a place to stay long term so need to waste any ink

A reservation is not required, you can come and go as you please

It's just a temporary set up until you find whatever it is you need

Just bricks formed together to keep you warm and block the rain

It's a house to live in while some think a home is just the same

Home is where the heart is, a place you receive everything you need

Stragglers no longer allowed in this home where that house use to be

Filled it up with permanent love and beautiful smiling faces

Removed old paintings, replaced the walls and furnished the empty spaces

Restarted the clocks and installed new locks on all the doors

This loving home will not allow squatters inside anymore

It's not just bricks formed together to keep you warm and block the rain

It's a heart filled with love, accepting happiness and rejecting unwanted pain

*7*rapped

Fighting to get off my knees after the struggle broke me down

Screaming at the top of my lungs for help refusing to hit the ground

Words speak volumes while actions tell the whole true story

No helping hands reaching down for me as my panicking turns to worry

No doors to break down or even a small window to crawl through

Trapped in the darkness without any lights to display a clear view

Breathing harder and faster as fear begins to take its place

Sweat and tears running full speed down my warm face

My hands are now free and no chains are attached to my feet

With a blurred vision a window is opened for me to see

A white door appears with no locks and no need for a key

Being held inside of some unknown place and needing to get myself free

Confused by the illusion as I wonder how this could be

The fear of being judged by others held me hostage inside of me

$\mathcal{F}$ather To Son

Reminiscing about the past and laughing about things I've done

Overcoming my failures and determined to teach the younger ones

Life is not a game and the struggle is sad but real

Stay focused on the positive and you'll never see the great bars of steel

I came from the bottom and I'm climbing my way to the top

Pushing for perfection while holding tight to everything I got

Mistakes have been made but great lessons were taught and learned

The fast lane may seem quick and easy but chances are you will get burned

Explore every option and make the best decision for you

Do not allow friends, family, anger, or fear determine what you think you can't do

At times I felt I failed you because of unknown circumstances

In time I knew I needed you and learned what a second chance is

A brighter future waits in front of you, grab ahold and don't let go

Learn the real ways of love and life and you will mature as you grow

The boy I was back then made me into the man I am today

Do better in life than I did and show others the right way

I left behind the mistakes I made as I pass on to you all the knowledge

Freshly laid cement with your footprints so those to follow can get to college

You are an intelligent and brave young man, no longer just a kid

March confidently into the future, don't stumble and fall the way I did

Look down at no one, always help up those in need

From a humbled father to a wonderful son, strive to do better and go further in life than me

roud Mother

Being a single mother was never an excuse

Failing or giving up was never an option to choose

Moving from house to house made jumping from school to school so hard

Saying keep your head held high and never let down your guard

Work hard, be determined and stay focused on success

Accept any challenge and fight with no fear to be your best

Cry your tears, lash out, but release the anger of not having a father around

Never let another person's decision hold you back or break you down

You are a beautiful blessing from God that I love more and more everyday

Beautiful, smart, sweet, innocent and intelligent in every way

From an adorable baby to a sneaky kid to a gorgeous woman with class

We can sit back now and laugh at all your drama and chaos from the past

Diploma in your hand filled with dreams of success full of realistic goals

You walked across the stage and every emotion inside of me showed

Happy, sad, excited, afraid, but most importantly proud

I can sit back and relax as you stand tall and gracefully take your bow

Being your mother is a job I will never complete

You have to live life now and walk the path designed for only your two feet

I Love You

hange

A change for better is what's happening to you

Loved by so many but only showed by a select few

Letting down your guard to allow others in

Showing compassion and understanding to your family and friends

Burying your past and giving birth to your future

Retracting your lies and revealing what your truth is

A change for better is what's happening to you

Looking at the world from someone else's view

Opening your heart and mind to something new

Feeling good on the inside with a new glow on your face

Showing appreciation to those that care and allowing them in your space

Being alone felt safe but in time all things change

Stepping out of your comfort zone with no doubt or shame

A change for better is what's happening to you

Grab ahold of everything life has to offer to you

Leave behind old baggage to lighten the weight

Rebuild the bonds that were not meant to break

Everyday time is lost that cannot be replaced

Rebuild the bonds that were not meant to break

A change for better is what's happening to you

But this change for better is a change for others too

Keep Your Head Up

Lift up your head young lady
take a deep breath then smile

Put your feet up and relax
you've concurred the first mile

It's a rough road I know
full of thunderstorms and tornados

Just watch how on this journey the clouds will part ways
then reveal a beautiful rainbow

The sun gone shine down so brightly on you

Stand still
be patient
watch what God will do

One chapter is closing
it is not the end

Pull out your pen and start writing
how this new chapter begins

The devil is waiting on you to give up and lose faith

God gave you a testimony
write it down as you give thanks

Keep Pushing

Searching for something that the eye can see

With full force and determination

Overlooking everything that surrounds me

As I hurry forward leaving behind my patience

Smiling with pride to the thoughts in my head

As the lights shine and the cameras flash

Remembering everything my sister said

As I grabbed my prize and took the cash

Be proud of your accomplishments

Put your doubters to shame

Don't leave them your butt to kiss

Intelligently thank them for your fame

The dreams you have are yours to keep

No man or woman can take them away

Continue forward until you reach your peak

Stand tall and be proud on the wonderful day

Me

Looking in the mirror with a smile on my face

Knowing my own beauty puts me in first place

Smooth brown skin with small dimples to show

Beautiful brown eyes with a cute petite nose

Fully shaped lips with a clear gloss

Silently repeating I am the boss

Knowing my worth and never doubting my strengths

Gives me the power to walk the full length

Head held high with confidence in every stride

Prepared to overcome all obstacles on this journey of mine

I am focused and determined to complete my goals

Never giving up on my dreams or accepting any no's

Looking in the mirror with a smile on my face

My beautiful mind is how I'm winning first place

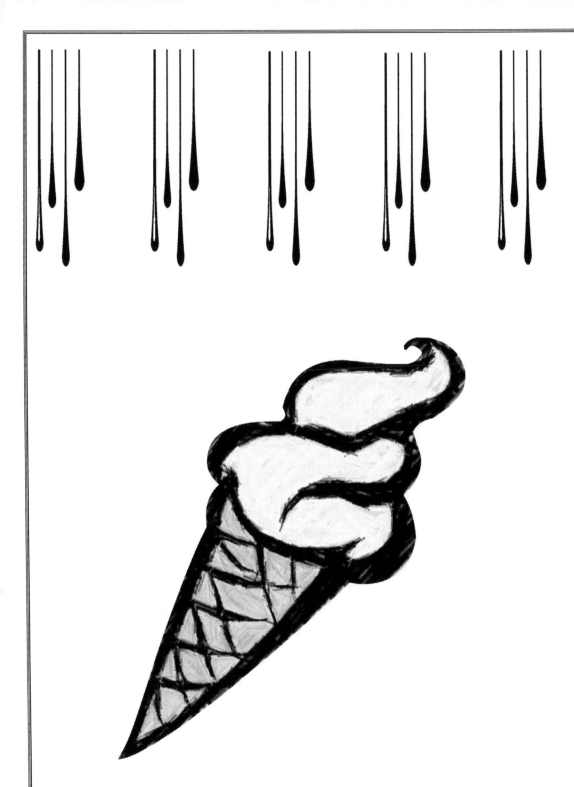

*W*hat's Your Flavor

Love is in the air, I can taste it

Sweet on my tongue and smooth on my lips

Cold to the touch as the sweetness drips

My body wants chocolate, rich and strong

Every time I get it I feel dirty and wrong

I'm a fein for your love, I need it twice a week

The way you get in my head I can hardly speak

Love is in the air, I can taste it

Licking my lips as you come my way

Wondering if this time you'll make me pay

Size doesn't matter it's the feeling I seek

Whenever I'm near you I feel like a freak

Red velvet, orange crush and carrot cake too

If I don't get my ice cream I don't know what I'll do

Dreams

Close your eyes
let's go to another place

Let me lead you soft and slowly
deep into my space

Let me kiss over your body
with my wet mouth and smooth lips

Juices start flowing
I'm catching every drip

Right there

Don't stop

Hold tight

Don't slip

I let you pull me in closer
holding tightly to my hips

I'm taking off clothing
piece by piece

As one we fall
down on our knees

Bottom raised high
cheeks spread, ready to please

Anticipating the pleasure
we both need

Standing tall and strong
as you enter my sweet spot

I'm throwing it back
giving it all I got

It feels so good
I let out a scream

Sweat dripping down my face
damn, it's just a dream....

Sexual

Gently placed kisses from my ear down to my neck
from his warm soft lips

Hushed moans of pleasure escape softly
as his hands roam my body and rest comfortably amongst my hips

Gently caressing his head as his mouth eagerly devours my breast

Softly he nibbles and licks my nipples
as his fingers ease slowly inside my nest

My hands slither slowly down his back
as his fingers massage my walls

I arch my back and spread my legs widely whispering, "I want it all"

Fingers covered with juicy sweetness sliding in and out my mouth

Shaking uncontrollably with pleasure and pain
as insertion caused a slight shout

Aggressively kissing, sucking, and biting my lips
as he slides deeper and deeper inside

Holding me tightly he rolls us over and sets me up to ride

Slow was my preference
as I maneuvered up and down his shaft

A feeling of pure ecstasy and pleasure
my body needed it to last

Both breast in his mouth
as his hands pull me down with each thrust

"Slow down Big Daddy, I need you in me all night, no need to rush"

I tighten my muscles with a naughty squeeze
as I lean back and ride, hands gripping his knees

Shaking fast as I grind and moan
releasing all my secrets with ease

Body tightening as he prepares to cum
I quickly open my mouth
as I drop to my knees

Wasted

Spinning in a circle with no brakes to stop

Head hurting worse with the sound of the clock

Light in my eyes reveal the red

Crawling slowly to find a place to rest my head

Straight no chaser only clear for me

Shot after shot of white Remy

Martini glass or a plastic cup

No, straight from the bottle, bottoms up

Jealous

Why you mad at my size three

My small waist and pedicured feet

Why you frowning at the way I walk

The way I sing and the way I talk

Why you questioning to whom I speak

As to why they think I'm so unique

Why are you so focused on me

The fun I have and the life I seek

Why can't you just live your life

Leave mine alone and get yours right

Smile

When you smile

The room forms a light

It gives hope that your present situation will get right

When you smile

The rain suddenly stops

A lovely rainbow appears as the sun shines about

When you smile

You show how beautiful you are

Prettier than the sun as bright as a star

When you smile

The world seems like a better place

A thousand people couldn't fill your space

When you smile

I smile

And the world smiles too

Mother

Cool and confident

Passionate and strong

The love from a mother never steers you wrong

Sassy mixed with class

Educated with strong beliefs

The love from a mother will land you on top never beneath

Quiet and mysterious

Happy never sad

The love from my mother is the love you wish you had

Powerful and demanding

Rich never poor

The love she gives leaves you wanting more

A mothers love is irreplaceable and always on time

The love from my mother is the love that's all mine

ather

Six foot tall

One hundred and ninety five pounds

Dark skinned complexion with dark brown eyes

Muscular built body with smooth skin

Honest and sincere

Calm and relaxed

A supporter, a provider, and a lover

A teacher, a friend, and a counselor

A hard worker and a brother

A husband and a father

A real man not a faker

A giver not a taker

A man

Not just any man

My father

*F*riends

Whenever I call you are always there

Giving me great support and advice

The guidance you give is filled with care

With an unbreakable bond that feels so nice

When I call you answer never leaving me alone

Allowing me to release my anger and fears

Silently listening on the phone

As I fight to hold back my tears

Late nights with food, fun, and drinks

Games and unbelievable stories

With you in my life I would never think

Of a better person to share my glory

Not just a friend to me but a sister in my heart

You are my best friend

In this life time we will never be apart

*H*eaven Awaits Me

Open the gates

cause here I come

For I lived my life for me and everyone

I have prepared my family for this wonderful day

For this life on earth I cannot stay

I have fought my battles and now they end

My new life in heaven shall now begin

Don't cry for me now or try to escape

For the memories we have cannot be erased

I raised you right and stood by your side

Now it's time for you to let me ride

My chariot has come to take me away

You must move forward and keep your faith

For God didn't judge me or make me suffer

He opened his arms and laid down his cover

For it is in heaven where I must rest

Always know that I gave you my best

The years to come will be hard I know

You have to keep moving, this is my time to go

*W*ings

Floating on a cloud up high in the sky

Watching tears fall from your saddened eyes

I blow them away with a gust of wind

Releasing sunshine so you can raise your chin

I am in heaven, a better place than earth

Smiling upon you like the day I gave you birth

My precious child I did not leave you alone

Stop crying those tears and saying I'm gone

I am here with you in every breath you breathe

You must understand that I had to leave

My body was tired and my soul was weak

I could not move but I could hear you speak

Hold tight to your life and all the wonderful things

Smile and be proud for I have received my wings

God's Angel

God has sent down for his angels

They have completed their job here on earth

All wings have been assigned and distributed

To us down here it seems unfair and it hurts

It may take some time to understand his reason

To remove so many loved ones at once

Only God knows what is best for this season

Though we feel it's all too soon and too much

Say I love you today while giving a hug or a kiss

Share some laughs and smile at good times

Tomorrow is not promised for any one of us

We do not know which one of Gods angels is next in line

*T*ears

The tears escape my eyes every time I think of you

Wishing you were near me

A song played on the radio and I sang with all my might

Wishing you could hear me

We laughed and joked and shared so many good times

Wishing we could do it once more

God called you home and I just wasn't ready

Wishing I could see you once more

We never actually said goodbye but I knew the time would come

I would have told you just how much I love you

And how you are the special one

My cousin, my friend, my sister in my heart

I am missing you like crazy

It seems like my world just fell apart

Selfishly I wanted you to stay

My heart knew you had to go

Heaven received a beautiful angel

I just wanted you to know

I love you

$\mathcal{P}$ray For Me

Hot and sweating started off this day

Anxiety attacks decided to come my way

Body filled with fear and sorrow

Wondering if I'll live to see tomorrow

Just as I came I have to go

These thoughts I have someone must know

Death is in my vision and I can't explain

These feelings I have hold so much pain

Crying through the night as dark shadows appear

For what does that mean, why are they here

Just as I came I have to go

These thoughts I have someone must know

Made in the USA
Lexington, KY
18 January 2017